CELEBRATING THE FAMILY NAME OF ZHANG

Celebrating the Family Name of Zhang

Walter the Educator

Silent King Books
a WhichHead Entertainment Imprint

Copyright © 2024 by Walter the Educator

All rights reserved. No part of this book may be reproduced in any manner whatsoever without written permission except in the case of brief quotations embodied in critical articles and reviews.

First Printing, 2024

Disclaimer

This book is a literary work; the story is not about specific persons, locations, situations, and/or circumstances unless mentioned in a historical context. Any resemblance to real persons, locations, situations, and/or circumstances is coincidental. This book is for entertainment and informational purposes only. The author and publisher offer this information without warranties expressed or implied. No matter the grounds, neither the author nor the publisher will be accountable for any losses, injuries, or other damages caused by the reader's use of this book. The use of this book acknowledges an understanding and acceptance of this disclaimer.

Celebrating the Family Name of Zhang is a memory book that belongs to the Celebrating Family Name Book Series by Walter the Educator. Collect them all and more books at WaltertheEducator.com

USE THE EXTRA SPACE TO DOCUMENT YOUR FAMILY MEMORIES THROUGHOUT THE YEARS

ZHANG

In the vast expanse where legends rise,

The name of Zhang reaches the skies.

A pillar strong, a timeless sound,

With roots so deep, in honor bound.

Born of earth and guided by stars,

The Zhang name travels near and far.

A lineage bold, both proud and wise,

Its stories written in endless skies.

From brush and ink to swords and steel,

The Zhangs pursue what's just and real.

Their voices echo through the past,

A name of courage, built to last.

Bamboo bends but does not break,

So too does Zhang the trials take.

With steadfast hearts and steady hands,

They shape the world, they guide the lands.

From scholars' pens to farmers' toil,

The Zhangs have nurtured sacred soil.

Through every field and mountain high,

Their legacy stands, it will not die.

Crafting futures with boundless might,

Dreamers by day, defenders by night.

A dynasty born of endless flame,

The Zhangs inspire, their deeds proclaim.

Each generation lifts the name,

Through winds of change, through joy and pain.

A family strong, its bond secure,

Through time eternal, they endure.

From painted scrolls to nature's art,

The Zhang name beats in every heart.

A melody of hope and pride,

A force that flows like ocean tides.

The seasons turn, the ages pass,

Yet Zhang endures, like tempered glass.

Their story woven in history's thread,

A name that lives, though years have fled.

So raise the banner, high and strong,

And sing of Zhang, their rightful song.

A name of honor, fierce and free,

A light for all eternity.

ABOUT THE CREATOR

Walter the Educator is one of the pseudonyms for Walter Anderson. Formally educated in Chemistry, Business, and Education, he is an educator, an author, a diverse entrepreneur, and he is the son of a disabled war veteran. "Walter the Educator" shares his time between educating and creating. He holds interests and owns several creative projects that entertain, enlighten, enhance, and educate, hoping to inspire and motivate you. Follow, find new works, and stay up to date with Walter the Educator™

at WaltertheEducator.com

www.ingramcontent.com/pod-product-compliance
Lightning Source LLC
LaVergne TN
LVHW052009060526
838201LV00059B/3933